RE-VISIONING

A ONE-DAY JOURNEY TO DISCOVER GOD'S VISION
FOR YOUR LIFE AND MINISTRY

AL NEWELL

Re-visioning: A One-Day Journey to Discover God's Vision for Your Life and Ministry

© 2016 by Al Newell

Edited by Suellen Sinclair Wenz

Cover and book design by Convertible

Printed in the United States of America

To my amazing Wendy, my courageous life, ministry and
Re-visioning partner. Wow—the journey of God we've discovered.
How beautiful to walk it with you.

CONTENTS

RE-VISIONING

Welcome to Re-visioning

···

"And if you seek Him, He will let you find Him."
(2 Chronicles 15:2 NASB)

THE NEED TO SEE CLEARLY

Leadville, Colorado, rises 12,000 feet in elevation. At that altitude, even summer nights get very chilly. I chose the small twin bed on the porch of the rustic cabin; thank God the kids chose sleeping bags on the floor. I took off my glasses, turned on my electric blanket, and fell fast asleep.

Brrr . . . I woke in the middle of the night — I had to use the bathroom. I groped for my glasses and began my trek to the other side of the cabin. Sleeping figures lay everywhere along the path. Like going through a minefield, I stumbled across the room, tripping over people and furniture. I stifled my tears and laughter!

Knowing I had made it to the other side of the room, the bathroom just a few feet away, I began to relax ever so slightly. That's when I slammed right into the bathroom door! I fumbled for the light switch only to hit a different button that started a loud, damaged fan! I slapped the wall until finally I found the light switch! The light came on, and the mirror in front of me revealed why my trek had been so difficult. I had put on my SUNGLASSES!

Sometimes my ability to see God's vision works like an excellent GPS system with no recalculating necessary, making it easier to lead both staff and volunteers, and making decision making so clear. Yet at other times, like my cabin trek, I seem to stumble in a general direction, hurting others and myself along the way. Oh, the importance of clear vision.

Maybe you are embarking on a new ministry venture and want to get off to a great start. Perhaps you have been in the same place for a while and your passion has waned. Maybe you and your spouse desire a clearer path for your life and/or for your family. Or perhaps you and your leadership team need a fresh view of what God would have you do. Maybe you simply understand the power of taking time away to sharpen your focus. Whatever your reason for Re-visioning, we thank God for your decision to go through this exercise.

David said, "O God, You are my God; I shall seek you earnestly" (Psalm 63:1 NASB). Re-visioning is all about attuning our hearts and ears to the counsel of God. Re-visioning emerged from a biblical practice that my wife, Wendy, and I have been developing and engaging in for over 20 years. I can't fully explain it, but God meets us each time as we Re-vision. God has used these simple exercises to reignite our hearts and deepen our passion. As a result, each year God's vision for each of our lives and ministries emerges anew right before our eyes.

So many years ago, we began sharing Re-visioning with other leaders who similarly experienced a profound impact on their personal lives and their leadership teams. Re-visioning principles are woven into all of our High Impact courses, which are taught to Christian leaders all over the world. As you will quickly see, the principles in Re-visioning are simply biblically based.

We hope and pray that, as it has been for so many, Re-visioning will be a profound experience infused with God's peace and presence, making clear His path for your life and ministry.

HOW TO USE THE RE-VISIONING RESOURCE

Re-visioning is a simple tool designed as a one-day event for individuals, couples, and leadership teams. You may desire, however, to complete this experience over a weekend or other extended time. This workbook will guide you through the simple journey we call Re-visioning. This workbook is for individual participants. If participating with your spouse, you'll want another booklet. If you plan to take your leadership team through this experience, you'll need booklets for every team member. **Visit www.newellandassociates.com to order extra *Re-visioning* booklets.**

For best results, successful Re-visioning requires getting to a quiet place with no distractions. In front of a fireplace, in the mountains, at the beach, or any retreat-type setting is perfect. Most have found it helpful to fast for a half or full day. After Wendy and I complete Re-visioning, we enjoy a very special dinner together. It's the perfect way to close out the special day.

WHEN YOU SEE...

 Further reflection on this scripture may light your path more clearly.

 This thought or question is worthy of deeper contemplation to guide your journey.

This is your space for writing responses. Recording your thoughts or feelings is crucial to Re-visioning. Use the allotted space. We've made sure to the leave the margins wide for jotting down any additional thoughts. Many will need additional paper. The key: Don't let anything keep you from expressing your thoughts or writing down key ideas or scriptures.

COMPLETING RE-VISIONING WITH YOUR SPOUSE OR A FRIEND

- Make sure you both have a copy of *Re-visioning*.
- Give yourselves an entire day or weekend to complete the experience.
- Pick a retreat-like spot where you will experience few distractions.
- You may want to read the *What Vision Is and Is Not* section in advance.
- After reading Step 1, pray together to get your journey off to a good start.
- Complete Step 2 individually. After 15-20 minutes, come back together to pray, worshipping and thanking God together for who He is and all He has done.
- Complete Steps 3-5 individually. Take about 30 minutes to an hour. Come back together to share and pray. It may not be appropriate or you may not feel comfortable sharing everything you've written in this area, even with your spouse. However, sharing as much as you are able will be immensely freeing and key to the rest of Re-visioning.
- Complete the remaining Steps 6-13 individually. Take several hours to complete these sections. Give yourself plenty of time to hear from God, especially during Step 9, *Hear God's voice through scripture.* Set a time later in the day to check in.
- Come back together and share all that God revealed to you. Take special note of common themes or scripture as God may be speaking the same ideas to both of you. If so, this may indicate confirmation of your direction.
- Complete the *Act Now!* section together.
- Wendy and I like to close Re-visioning with a dinner that allows our conversation to continue. Try to do this with your partner if possible.

LEADING YOUR TEAM THROUGH RE-VISIONING

- For best results, first complete Re-visioning by yourself.
- Make sure each team member has a workbook.
- Assign each team member a Re-visioning partner (same gender). Pray for God's leading to ensure the best matches. It is crucial that each participant feel comfortable and safe sharing with his or her partner.
- You may want to start your day in worship. Encourage participants not only to seek God for their individual lives, but also for direction with regard to your ministry together.
- FOLLOW THE ADVICE ON THE PREVIOUS PAGE: *Completing Re-visioning with your spouse or a friend.*
- Toward the end of the day, bring everyone back together for at least an hour. Have people sit with their partners. The Re-visioning experience can create a very sensitive environment. Some team members may have experienced something very powerful that may have evoked deep feelings. It is important to create a very safe environment—one in which people can share their experience without feeling a threat of judgment. Set the stage by defining this time as an opportunity for participants to share what they experienced, not a time for discussion or debates. Make it clear that sharing is optional. Be patient, allowing ample time for people to respond, as the reflective experience may cause people to be hesitant to respond immediately. People *will* respond. Here are some discussion questions you may find helpful:
  + What was this experience like for you?
  + What did you learn?
  + Did you feel strongly that God supernaturally reminded you of or directed you to specific scripture? If so, would you be willing to share?
  + Did you sense God gave you clarity in an area of your life? Or in your specific ministry?
  + Did you feel or learn anything specific regarding our ministry as a whole? (Stay clear of debates.)

- Have team members complete the *Act Now!* step. Schedule a follow-up meeting to discuss next steps.
- Conclude the Re-visioning experience with a dinner together.

....

"And if you seek Him, He will let you find Him."
(2 Chronicles 15:2 NASB)

....

RE-VISIONING

What Vision Is and Is Not

Before you journey through the specific steps of Re-visioning, it may be helpful to understand our definition of *vision*. So whether or not you agree with our definition, at least you will understand our point of reference.

Let's first look at some common misunderstandings about vision.

VISION IS NOT BASED ON FEELING

In Ezekiel 13:1-16 (ESV), God commands Ezekiel to speak against the false prophets who prophesy from *their own hearts, or inspiration* (v. 2). "Woe to the foolish prophets who follow their own spirit and have seen nothing" (v. 3). "They have seen false visions . . . the Lord has not sent them, and yet they expect him to fulfill their word" (v. 6). Also in Jeremiah 14:13-14, many prophets were saying that Jerusalem *would not see famine or the sword and would have lasting peace*. But through Jeremiah the Lord said these were false prophets with false visions made by the "deception of their own minds [hearts]" (NASB). It is common for people to "feel" they have God's direction or "vision" when they definitely do not.

VISION IS NOT MAJORITY RULE.

God's direction or vision is not always understood by the majority. Often in many Western or democratic societies, majority support aids major decision making. In scriptures, the majority often support false visions. Many times, maybe most of the time, false prophets outnumber the true ones. Hundreds of false prophets stood opposite Elijah at Mt. Carmel, yet only Elijah heard God's voice clearly. Joshua and Caleb grasped God's vision for the Promised Land, while the other 10 spies saw only obstacles (Numbers 13). And how often did the entire congregation turn against Moses, the one man who spoke face to face with God?

God's vision is often grasped by the minority.

VISION SHOULD NEVER ORIGINATE AS A RESPONSE TO NEEDS

It is a mistake to determine God's vision based on needs. Unsure of whether or not God might be directing Wendy and me to start a church, I had lunch with a friend. I shared what I thought might be God's direction with Dr. Alemu Beeftu, a native of Ethiopia, and founder and president of Gospel of Glory. He asked me, "Al, why do you want to start a church?" I shared that so many people were deeply hurting and I felt God could use me to meet their compelling needs. Alemu gently corrected my thinking: "Al, we never start a ministry based on need, but only as a result of God's calling." He was so right!

It is common for people to "feel" they have God's "vision" when they definitely do not.

The world's needs are limitless and overwhelming, and it's right and natural that a follower of Christ with a heart for others would want to respond tangibly to these hardships. Christian leaders, however, must trust that God knows how best to approach crushing needs around the globe. As a consultant to Christian leaders for more than 20 years, I have seen compassionate leaders responding to endless needs and straying from the course of God's focused direction. We can best help those in need when we are anchored to God's clear vision, not the shifting sand of infinite needs.

With that as a backdrop, let's talk about vision.

WHAT THEN IS VISION?

Our High Impact definition of vision is *a God-given picture of the future that you and/or your organization are called to fulfill.*

If I can clearly see exactly what God has for my family, our organization, or me, then I can move toward that vision with great conviction, greater ease, and more effectiveness. In addition, as a leader, the clearer I understand God's vision, the more compelling my message will be in inviting staff and volunteers to follow.

In High Impact, everything starts with a God-driven vision. With the High Impact definition of vision in mind, let's look at eight biblical principles related to vision.

1. Vision is God driven — that is, initiated by God and discovered by us.

Think of this: Jesus, the Lord of Lords, *did nothing on His own initiative.* John 8:28

A company's CEO led prominent international visitors on a tour throughout his organization's entire campus. Although many parts of the campus stood out, one unusual aspect of each building drew particular praise from the tour group. "How do you keep the stairs in each building looking so spotless?" the group wanted to know. "They are beautiful; each step is so clean." The company executive, pleasantly surprised by the group's admiration, contacted the man responsible for the stairs and asked him to reveal his secret. "The secret," he responded, "is that I simply clean the stairs exactly the way I was taught on the very first day I arrived. I do it every day."

A couple of scripture passages catch me completely off guard. In John 8:28, Jesus says something shocking: "I do nothing on My own initiative, but I speak these things as the Father taught me" (NASB). Then again in John 14:10: "The words I say to you I do not speak on My own initiative, but the Father abiding in Me does His works."

Jesus, the Savior, the Lord of Lords, did *nothing* on His own initiative. His actions, behaviors, and His entire life mission did not emanate from a great idea, a momentary insight. They were not an attempt to create

His own destiny; *He did nothing* on His own initiative. His words, His miracles, and His teaching rose up from the heart of His Father. They were ultimately the purposes of God. Jesus, like the man who took care of the beautiful stairs, simply was faithful, obedient to every detail of God's revealed plan. How much more should I, should we, *seek God* for His plans and directions for His ministry.

An oft-repeated phrase in Exodus reveals much the same truth about Moses: "According to all that the Lord commanded him, so he did." In Exodus 39 and 40 (NASB) this phrase or a variation of this phrase is used more than 10 times. Moses did exactly as he was commanded in putting together every detail of the Tabernacle. When it comes to vision, naturally I want to dream big. I want the plans for next year to emanate from a profound thought of *mine*. Not so with Jesus, or Moses. They received vision, direction, and the details of their mission from God.

Our job in Re-visioning is to *discover God's vision,* not come up with our own. As we mentioned earlier, vision that has its impetus from our feelings or our own initiative is dangerous.

2. God-given vision is consistent with God's Word.
Deuteronomy 13:1 and following says that even if a wonder or supernatural sign accompanies a prophet or dreamer's picture of the future, we are not to listen if it contradicts God's law. If your vision contradicts God's previously revealed Word, it is not of God. A pastor once informed me that God clearly told him it was okay to divorce his wife and marry another woman. His wife had done nothing worthy of divorce. What that pastor heard was not of God.

Sometimes our feelings cause us to act outside of God's will. The apostle Paul in Galatians 1:8, 9 teaches that even if an angel of God should preach a different gospel, let him be accursed, i.e., separated from God. According to Psalm 1, he who meditates day and night on God's Word is like a tree firmly planted by streams of water, yielding its fruit. The strength, durability, and fruitfulness of your vision will correlate positively to its alignment with God's Word.

Our job is to discover God's vision, not come up with a new one.

The durability and fruitfulness of your vision will correlate positively to its alignment to God's Word.

3. We are responsible to test the vision or picture of the future we see to make sure it is from God.

Knowing our weakness and humanness, we are to test any vision, teaching, or prophecy to see if it is from God. In 1 Thessalonians 5:19-21, Paul tells the Thessalonians not to quench the Spirit or hate prophetic utterances, but to *test* or examine each one. In 1 John 4:1, we are commanded not to believe every spirit but to *test the spirits* to see if they are from God. The Greek word for *test* in both passages — *dokimadzo* — means to approve after evaluation. It's a word also used in the testing of metals. Comparing our vision to God's previously revealed Word is a clear way to test to see if it is God's vision.

In addition, God wants us to use the reasoning skills He has given us to evaluate or test a vision. Fulfillment or non-fulfillment of a prophecy is a sure test. In Deuteronomy 18, the Old Testament law shows how serious it is to claim to speak for God. Verses 20-22 say that if a prophet presumes to speak in God's name and in fact the word did not come from God, that person would die. Also verse 22 shows that we are not to fear or respect the prophet whose prophecy does not become a reality.

4. God's vision is accompanied by His provision.

Where God guides, He provides resources to accomplish His vision. Hudson Taylor, pioneer missionary and founder of the China Inland Mission, may have said it best: "God's work done in God's way will never lack God's supply." Be assured that if it is God's vision, it will happen. The Apostle Paul assures the Thessalonians, "Faithful is He who calls you, and He also will bring it to pass" (1 Thessalonians 5:24, NASB). Though the specific context is holiness, I've found it to be true of any endeavor initiated by God.

In 1992, through a number of answered prayers and some supernatural confirmations, Wendy and I sensed God's clear calling to leave Compassion International by faith and start the ministry of Newell and Associates: High Impact Volunteer Ministry Development. In the midst of a struggling economy, and surrounded by the doubt of some friends and family, I stood strongly on the promise of 1 Thessalonians 5:24. Yet my faith was tempered with the reality that it is easy to mistake God's voice. We left Compassion August 1 and had enough money to make it for three months. I told Wendy that if God did not provide by the time our money ran out on October 31, I would look for a job. During the last days of October, God provided just enough income so that we felt directed to set another deadline of December 31. Supernaturally, God provided again. Our first long-term client came on December 29! From that day forward, God has met our needs with His provision, confirming without a doubt His vision for this ministry. Where God guides, He provides His resources.

5. God's vision requires risk and steps of faith.
Hebrews 11:6 says it is impossible to please God without faith. God's vision often extends beyond the human limitations of sight and often reaches toward impossibility. God is a supernatural God and wants to show us how much He loves us and how great He is. God is pleased by faith. In response to God's vision, Moses said to God, "Who am I that I should go to Pharaoh and bring the children of Israel out of Egypt?" (Exodus 3:11, ESV). The person or team who hears and sees God's vision may be overwhelmed. When I compare the enormous vision that God has given me with my "five loaves and two fish," I am often overwhelmed. Then I am reminded that God desires we acknowledge the enormous gap between His vision and our resources, that we admit our weakness, and rely on His power and presence for the vision to be realized.

God's vision extends beyond human capacity.

6. Accomplishing God's vision will mean encountering opposition.
The day Samuel anointed David, the young shepherd, to be king, God declared His vision for David. Long before the vision of royalty was realized, David experienced hate from his brother (1 Samuel 17:28, 29), a battle with Goliath (1 Samuel 17), and many attempts by King Saul to kill him (1 Samuel 18-20). In Acts 9:15 ff., God not only reveals His vision for Paul to bring the gospel to the Gentiles, but also indicates that much suffering would accompany Paul's journey. Many of God's servants experienced personal suffering and opposition from within and without. As Paul reminds us in Ephesians 6, physical hindrances are symptoms of the much greater spiritual forces that oppose God's work.

Many times Christian leaders will have a great vision to apply High Impact principles in the development of their volunteer ministries. They seem surprised when they encounter resistance. Yet can you recall a great work of God that did not encounter regular opposition? Achieving God's vision with God's power will mean hard work and suffering amidst opposition. Opposition may in fact indicate you're on the right track. You may finish your Re-visioning time with great joy, seeing clearly God's picture for your future, but be assured the evil one will look to destroy it and may work hard to keep your boat at the dock.

7. God's vision will produce spiritual fruit.
Another proof of God's call or vision is that we will see progress or fruit so long as we walk in faith. Moses did in fact build the Tabernacle with the people of God! Joshua did take possession of the Promised Land. David became a great shepherd as king of God's people. Nehemiah rebuilt the walls of Jerusalem. Countless Gentiles came to Christ, confirming God's vision for Paul. While God's vision through Nehemiah was realized in a mere 52 days, other works of God took far longer. Scholars estimate David did not officially become king of Judah until age 30, many years after Samuel first anointed him (1 Samuel 16:10-13). He had to wait another seven and a half years to reign over a united Israel (2 Samuel 5:4-5).

Fruit and nut trees can take four, six, eight, or even ten years to produce edible fruit. Years ago, Sue, a longtime friend and prayer partner, planted a lemon tree from a seed in her backyard. Now 20 years later, that tree is prolific. While it may take a while to see ultimate outcomes of God's vision realized, be assured you will see some progress — even if only a sprout — along the way. If it is God's picture of the future, be assured it will come about!

8. God often times delivers His vision in the context of intimacy or brokenness.

God is near to the brokenhearted and saves those who are crushed in spirit (Psalm 34:18). When I am at a low point or when my sins show me how disgusting I am, and just when my heart is filled with the knowledge of my failures, God reveals His vision in the midst of my brokenness. In 1 Chronicles 21 and 22 (cf. 2 Samuel 24), David conducted a census. Some of the details are unclear, yet it *is* clear that David knew he sinned egregiously by handling the census in the way he did. "I have sinned greatly . . . please take away the iniquity of your servant" (1 Chronicles 21:8 ESV). God spoke through Gad, David's seer, and offered David three terrible choices for severe discipline. Because of David's choice, an angel of God destroyed 70,000 of Israel's men. 1 Chronicles 21:16-17 describes how David and the elders in sackcloth and ashes could visually see the angel of the Lord and fell on their faces.

"You will find Him, if you search for Him with all your heart and with all your soul." Deuteronomy 4:29 (ESV)

These verses reveal David's brokenness and surrender. It was at this time at the very place where the angel of God had reached out his hand that **God revealed His vision**. The place was the threshing floor of Ornan. David purchased the land and built an altar, the very place of his terror, the place where he fully surrendered his heart and re-engaged with God. God revealed His vision further by giving very specific plans for how the temple was to be built. This very location is where Solomon built the temple according to God's plan. What a powerful, beautiful story of redemption.

"And if you seek Him, He will let you find Him."
(2 Chronicles 15:15 NASB)

*With all of this as a backdrop, let's begin
the Re-visioning process.*

OPEN YOUR HEART
TO RE-VISIONING

Every person who seeks a therapist, every patient who consults a doctor, and every traveler who requests directions from a local — all share a common disposition: a humility, an openness to a deeper understanding of themselves, their journey, or both.

"Then I turned my face to the Lord God, seeking him by prayer and pleas for mercy with fasting and sackcloth and ashes." (Daniel 9:3 ESV)

RE-VISIONING

Step 1. Set your focus to *seek God with all your heart.*

....

SETTING OUR HEARTS TO SEEK GOD

Scripture assures us that if we seek God, we will find Him. In 2 Chronicles 15:2 (NASB), Azariah the prophet spoke God's Word to King Asa and to all Judah and Benjamin: "The Lord is with you while you are with him. And if you seek Him, He will let you find Him." Deuteronomy 4:29 (ESV) says, "But from there you will seek the Lord your God and you will find him, if you search after Him with all your heart and with all your soul."

SETTING OUR HEARTS TO SEEK

Could there be a better promise? In James 4:8 (ESV), God's Word puts forth a powerful promise, "Draw near to God and He will draw near to you." The late J. Oswald Sanders, former General Director of OMF (Overseas Missionary Fellowship, China Inland Mission) in his Leadership series comments on this powerful promise of reciprocity: "We are not as close to God as we wish to be or desire to be; we are as close to God as we **choose** to be."

There are two reasons why we seek: (1) We become aware that we have lost something, or (2) We realize that there is something great to be found, a treasure.

Wendy and I frequently drive to our ministry destinations with a truckload of equipment. Because of our schedules, one works while the other drives. One day I pulled over so Wendy could drive and I could start a phone meeting. Somewhere in the transfer, my cell phone disappeared. I panicked! I started tearing apart our Sequoia.

Think for a moment. Have you ever lost your keys, cell phone, wallet, or other important item? Can you recall the frantic search that ensued? Yet it's interesting that sometimes an important item is lost for days before we realize it. We're not in a panic, not on a search, because as far as we know, nothing is lost.

How frantic is your search for a lost cell phone?

A few years back I remember reading Revelation 2 and believing clearly that God was speaking to me, that I had left my *first love*. Just like in scripture, He was pleased with me doing many good things, but this was simply God's assessment of me: "You've left your first love." My response: "Not me Lord, I walk close with you. Not me Lord, look at all I do." God was gently trying to tell me I had lost something, and I was not even aware that it was lost.

The second reason we seek is to find something greater. Once while we were training at a conference in Cincinnati, a friend took us to an incredible ice-cream shop. I had to experience more, so I returned every night during my entire stay.

In 2 Chronicles 15:2 and 15, the word *seek* translates two different Hebrew words. Both words imply searching or pursuing God, especially in prayer or worship. In Psalm 63:1 (ESV), David says, "O God, you are my God; earnestly I seek you; my soul thirsts for you; my flesh faints for you." The Hebrew for "earnestly I seek You" conveys the idea of rising early to search for something. It also conveys the notion of a painstaking, ardent search. To show the intensity of his desire, David also uses the words "thirst" and "faint."

David was on a constant journey to experience more of God. The parts he knew of God were so great, he couldn't get enough. His hunger and thirst could not be quenched. Like my repeated trip to the ice-cream shop, he had to return for more and more.

The first part of Re-visioning is seeking God with all of your heart, and initially this means to set your heart to seek. Maybe it's clear that you've lost something. Perhaps the sweetness of your relationship with God has waned; maybe you know it or like me you're too "spiritual" to accept it. Maybe the experience with your current ministry team lacks something it once had. So perhaps you're Re-visioning and seeking because you've lost something, or maybe you are ready to seek because you keep experiencing more of God and you must return and get more and more. **Whatever the case, set your heart in the direction to seek God.**

The second part of seeking God with all your heart is to *seek God and the truth.* What if you ask God for specific direction or wisdom and He gives it to you? Imagine the prophet Isaiah in Isaiah 6, his heart broken, his spirit willing: "I'll do whatever you want. Here I am, Lord." "Okay," God says. "Your job is to go and preach a harsh message to every congregation; tell them they are dull to God's Word and deaf spiritually."

I can almost hear Isaiah saying, "Hmmm . . . Lord, are there any other jobs I could do?"

In Jeremiah 42:3, the people, a remnant of Judah, sought to hear from God as to whether they should remain in Judah under the king of Babylon or leave and gain shelter in Egypt. In verse 6 they promised, "Whether it is pleasant or unpleasant we will listen to the voice of the Lord" (NASB). Jeremiah vowed to tell them exactly what the Lord told him. So he sought God for 10 days. At the end of 10 days, God told Jeremiah clearly that they should stay in Judah and they would be safe. The scripture reports in chapter 43:1, 2 that as soon as Jeremiah finished speaking, a key leader and a number of others said, "You are lying. God didn't tell you that. You are only saying that because someone else who hates us told you to tell us that" (my paraphrase).

Do you really want to hear God? The truth? I often don't really desire to hear the truth.

In some of our trainings, we have attendees complete a "blind spots" exercise where participants invite coworkers, family, and friends to share leadership or character flaws that may be hindering their leader's capacity for kingdom building. The leader invites others to share the truth but is not allowed to respond to the commenter, thus making the exercise very safe for commenters. I've been doing this exercise for years. When I started, it was the most painful exercise I'd ever participated in. Yet now I know it is the most wonderful exercise.

Do you hunger to see God's vision? What if, as we proceed, God reveals to you something in your personal theology, belief system, or team philosophy that is actually hindering His plan for you? Are you tied to an unhealthy tradition? Would you be willing to go through some chaos in order to gain greater health, freedom, and effectiveness for Jesus?

In Acts 10, God violently shook the Apostle Peter's entire theological world when through a vision, God told this Jewish man with deeply held traditions to go ahead and eat "unclean" foods. This was hard for

Peter, but he heard God's truth. To fully understand God's complete vision for the future, Peter's thinking had to fundamentally change.

In Acts 10 God violently shook Peter's entire theological world.

For so long I rejected every confusing Bible verse that departed from my own narrow systematic theology. I would interpret a text so that it would fit my theology. Today I just want to know the truth. I want to know what Jesus believes on every issue. I study the Bible today with a fear of God, with the attitude that I want to know the truth of the Living God — and wow, the freedom, the beauty, the consistency in the Word.

As you go forward, may I encourage you to seek God's truth, be a bit vulnerable, and not be afraid of the truth about yourself or your organization. It may "ouch" a little, but oh, the healing. We can't experience the healing salve of Jesus unless we show Him where it hurts.

For some people, becoming vulnerable is awkward — like wearing a hospital gown. I think I know why in the Old Testament so many people made their trek to get closer to God wearing sackcloth and covering themselves with ashes. If you tend to insulate yourself from vulnerability, may I ask you to do your best to try to be open?

Lastly, as you seek God to refine your vision, seek God with all of your heart.

WHAT IS THE HEART?

In the Bible, both the Hebrew and Greek word for *heart* has two meanings. (1) The first meaning is simply the physical heart. (2) The second meaning in both languages represents the spiritual heart, the very center of our being, including the emotions, the mind, and the will. It's where our deepest motives reside. It's the real us, the "true self," no matter what we want people to believe. God looks at my heart because He knows that's the real me. He isn't fooled as other people are by the person I present to them. No, my Father God sees the real me better than I see myself.

A healthy physical heart results in great circulation, creating lots of energy. On the other hand, shortness of breath, a sore throat, and poor energy may indicate an unhealthy heart. Just as the physical heart is central to human health, so our spiritual heart is deeply connected and central to our spiritual health.

In Matthew 15:18-19 (NASB), Jesus said, "The things that proceed out of the mouth come from the heart. . . . For out of the heart come evil thoughts, murders, adulteries, fornications, thefts, false witness, slanders." Good and bad thoughts, encouraging and hateful words, righteous and evil actions are all generated from our heart. My ability to bear fruit starts with my heart. The heart is central to effective individual and team ministry, and it's from the heart we see the vision of God.

We grasp God's vision with the eyes of our heart by faith. "Blessed are the pure in heart for they shall see God" (Matthew 5:8 ESV). If our heart is unhealthy, we cannot see the things of God. In Numbers 13, Joshua and Caleb, two of 12 selected to spy out the Promised Land, were optimistic about this new place. Seeing with the eyes of faith, Caleb proclaimed, "We should by all means go up and take possession of it" (Numbers 13:30 NASB). However, the 10 other spies, seeing the same physical facts, saw huge opposing people and a land that *devoured its inhabitants.* They spread the doubt throughout all of Israel. Something was wrong with their hearts.

Jeremiah 17:9 gives us insight into the condition of the heart: "The heart is more deceitful than all else and is desperately sick; who can understand it?" (NASB). The heart has a bent toward evil, denial, and self-deception. Through faith in Christ, our heart is regenerated, though constantly at war with the remnants of the old heart forever trying to return us to denial and self-deception. Our new heart or spirit is eager to seek God. The new spirit is eager for truth and honesty, and works to uncover layers of self-deceit, trying to uncover the "true self" and unmask evil motives, making us holy in the process.

We grasp God's vision with the eyes of our heart.

The purer our heart — that is, the more we entrust the healing of our heart to God — the clearer our spiritual vision is.

What does it mean to seek God with all of your heart? Jeremiah 29:13 says that the people would find God when they searched for Him with all of their heart.

Having returned from a quiet dinner, Wendy and I were sitting and talking when Wendy glanced at her hand and gasped, "My diamond is gone." She held her hand so that I could see the empty mount. *My diamond is gone.* Those words immediately transformed the evening. One moment we were relaxed; the very next we were scrambling to find the diamond. We had no idea of when or where we lost it. We frantically retraced our steps and cried out to God until we finally found it in our carpet.

Our energies were focused on finding that diamond. We were searching with everything we had. We were urgent, even desperate. That's what it's like to seek God with all of our heart. Seeking God with all of our heart means a focused, urgent search with no distractions.

May I encourage you to let nothing compete with your trek to seek God today? If you are trying to complete the Re-visioning exercise with all of your children present, or if your cell phone is active, or you are worried about "a big game," may I encourage you to take a moment and clear your mind? Set you heart to focus and urgently seek for God and to do so with an undivided heart.

You will find God when you search for Him with all your heart.
Jeremiah 29:13

Prayer: I pray, God, that You would give me undivided focus to seek You. God, I ask that You would make me open, even vulnerable to whatever You have for me. I pray, God, that You will use this time to give me a crystal-clear, unmistakable vision for what You would have me to do. Please help me to spend as much time as You would like me to on each step. Please keep evil and distractions away from me during this time. Help me to seek You with my whole heart.

RESPONSE

Seek God:
1. Stop doing and thinking about something else.
2. Take several minutes now to get rid of distractions. Unpeel your hand from your cell phone and, if possible, shut it down.
3. Make a commitment not to rush the experience or be on a strict timetable.
4. Take a few moments to pray (something like the prayer above).

The first step of Re-visioning is a decision to seek God with all of your heart. Now each subsequent step of the process requires participation.

RE-VISIONING

Step 2. Allow yourself to become overwhelmed with God's greatness.

ASK GOD TO OPEN YOUR HEART'S EYES

In 2 Kings 6, through supernatural revelations, Elisha frustrated the war plans of the king of Aram in his attempts to defeat the king of Israel. The king of Aram saw Elisha as a spiritual pest and desperately tried to get rid of him. In 2 Kings 6:14-17 (NASB), the king of Aram sent horses and chariots and a great army by night to surround the city of Dothan where Elisha was. In the morning, Elisha's attendant woke up early and went outside. There he witnessed an entire army surrounding the city and in great fear cried out for Elisha, "Alas, my master! What shall we do?" (v. 15).

Elisha calmed his servant with these revealing words, "Do not fear, for those who are with us are more than those who are with them" (v. 16). Then Elisha prayed, "O Lord, I pray, open his eyes that he may see" (v. 17). And the Lord did. And the servant saw that the mountain was full of a supernatural army — horses and chariots of fire there to protect Elisha and his servant. It took a special set of spiritual eyes to see beyond the physical to the ultimate reality.

Like the hidden heavenly army, often God's greatness remains hidden from my sight just beneath the surface of the army of negative circumstances that surround me. God is great all the time, right? Why am I not grateful and not more readily enamored with His greatness? Could it be that I have a heart problem? Perhaps callousness keeps my heart from seeing God's greatness.

In Isaiah 6, God reveals a great vision to Isaiah in which God gives him a clear mission for his life. It begins with Isaiah becoming overwhelmed with God's greatness: "I saw the Lord . . . lofty and exalted, with the train of His robe filling the temple. Seraphim stood above Him. . . . And one called out to another and said, 'Holy, Holy, Holy, is the Lord of hosts.' . . . And the foundations of the thresholds trembled at the voice of him who called out, while the temple was filling with smoke" (vs. 1-4 NASB).

Wow!!! If you and I were taken into the presence of God like that, we would fall down and begin worshiping God! It's something we would never forget.

There are times when God answers a prayer so specifically, His power is made so clear, or His Word jumps off the page so dramatically that I experience His presence powerfully and I am overcome with gratefulness and **overwhelmed by His greatness.** What keeps me from that experience all the time? Poor eyesight. Like Elisha's servant, the eyes of my heart are unable to see. Let me share with you two conditions that have hurt my eyesight: ungratefulness and a poor memory.

Ungratefulness and a poor memory block the lenses of my heart.

PRACTICE GRATEFULNESS AND AFFIRMATION

Oh, the potency of a grateful heart. It reveals its influence in all relationships. Imagine how much greater marriages would be if spouses were simply more affirming. How much sweeter would families be? How many broken ministry and work relationships could be avoided if we were simply more grateful?

When my daughter Becky was a teen, there was a time that our relationship turned ugly. Every time Becky returned from school, I met her with sternness. She disrespected me, might talk under her breath, and would leave defiant. The cycle spun out of control until one day it occurred to me: *How would I like to come home to me? How would I like being greeted with sternness and demands?* So the next day I met Becky with a smile and words of affirmation. She returned my words with a gracious response. Almost immediately, **bitterness left my heart**. Love and gratefulness filled it. A big part of the problem had been me. I could have lost Becky, but now with my new set of eyes my heart was reminded of what an incredible daughter I have. Wow, how I wish all relational conflicts could be solved so simply.

"Enter His gates with thanksgiving."
Psalm 100:4 (ESV)

What one of us does not enjoy and need genuine affirmation? I don't want flippant affirmation or disingenuous praise from others, but how it lifts my spirit for someone to acknowledge my sacrifice or my worth. *You noticed — great!*

It's no wonder the writer says in Psalm 100, "Come into His presence with singing! . . . Enter his gates with thanksgiving, and his courts with praise!" (v. 2, 4 ESV). When we enter His door, His gates, when we enter into communication with Him, He desires we start with thanksgiving and praise! Because He knows their impact on our hearts.

Since we likely will not be transported into God's heavenly temple as Isaiah was, let's enter God's presence by taking the next step of Re-visioning — focusing on thankfulness. It's a great way to refresh our memories. May this step begin to open the eyes of our heart and give us a glimpse of and help us to magnify **the greatness of our God.**

RECALL SPECIFIC THINGS AND EVENTS
FOR WHICH TO BE THANKFUL

In order to appreciate God's greatness, Wendy and I begin with a thankfulness exercise. We begin to write down as fast as we can all we have to be thankful for in the last year, both in our personal lives and in the ministry. When we begin to do this, it is amazing how quickly we realize how much we've forgotten about the truly amazing things God has done. I can't stop writing. Five items turn into 10. One thing reminds me of another and soon I have 20, 30, 50 things flooding my mind, reaffirming what God has really done! When I compare my list with Wendy's I am even more amazed and even ashamed that I have forgotten other incredible things He's done and that I am not more grateful.

Sample prayer: Thank You, God, that I didn't run out of gas on the highway. Thank You, God, for healing my wife of cancer miraculously. Thank You, God, for the good report from the doctor. Thank You, God, for our children. Thank You, God, for the way You supernaturally orchestrated the entire event to work out when I was so worried. Thank You, God, that our children have jobs. Thank You for our grandchildren. Thank You, God, for Your Word and the amazing passage you gave me. Thank You for the many who came to Jesus on Sunday. Thank You for my prayer team. Thank You that You have blessed our business. Thank You for the special time we had at Christmas. Thank You for the abundance of food I have every day. Thank You for sustaining my daughter and her baby through a rough pregnancy. Thank You, God, for the amazing beauty of the ocean, the mountains, the lakes, the horizon. Thank You for the opportunity to share the gospel. Thank You for . . . I go on and on and on . . . .

RESPONSE

Let's enter this door, the next step of Re-visioning, with thankfulness.
Take some time now to write down as fast as you can everything that
God has done for you or things you have to be thankful for in the
past year. Spend 10 to 15 minutes or so writing these down, and
another 10 or so personally thanking God for each one.

OVERCOME OBSTACLES TO SPIRITUAL HEALTH

We've been reminded of how great our God is, so let's take the next step in Re-visioning. This step requires us to undergo a sort of exploratory procedure. Heart specialists employ a process called cardiac catheterization, which allows them to diagnose and treat heart problems. Using this procedure, physicians are not only able to detect how badly arteries are blocked, but often they are able to use the procedure to help increase blood flow.

Blocked spiritual arteries can decrease spiritual blood flow.

Blocked "arteries" also can decrease spiritual "blood flow," blurring or dulling our ability to see God's vision clearly. Let's allow God to direct His scope into our spiritual arteries and look at three common "blockages": callousness to personal sin, dullness to corporate sin, and unidentified fears.

Let's look now at the first possible blockage that may hinder our spiritual circulation and cloud our vision: sin.

RE-VISIONING

Step 3. Identify and confess your sins to God.

Luke 5:1-11 details the calling of Peter. Having spent the entire previous night fishing with no success, Peter is not anxious to go out again. However, at Jesus' request he takes the boat into the deep, lets down his nets, and experiences a miraculous catch. Peter, James, and John are awed and amazed. Peter realizes this display of supernatural power has less to do with Jesus' concern for fishing and far more to do with the greatness of God that is in Jesus! Overwhelmed by God's power, Peter falls down at Jesus' feet and with humility cries, "Go away from me Lord, for I am a sinful man!" (v. 8 NASB). The nearer we get to God, the more clearly our sinfulness and unworthiness come into view.

RECOGNIZE AND CONFESS PERSONAL SIN

In Isaiah 6:5 (NASB), just following Isaiah's description of the powerful heavenly vision of angels, he similarly confesses: "Woe is me, for I am ruined! Because I am a man of unclean lips, and I live among a people of unclean lips; For my eyes have seen the King, the Lord of hosts."

As a teen I worked summers at Cineks, my dad's chicken distribution business. Among other things, I trimmed fat off chickens going to restaurants. One day my hand slipped and a razor-sharp knife sliced my thumb deeply. At the hospital, the nurse holding a long needle said that before they could stitch me up, they would need to numb the area with Novocain. Evidently my thumb was sensitive, because with each of the four injections, I had to stifle my screams. Tears welled up. To this day, there is a scar across my thumb and, as sensitive as my thumb is, there is absolutely no feeling where the scar is. Scars damage our sensitivity. Unconfessed sin callouses or scars our heart and reduces our ability to hear God's voice and sense His Spirit.

The Greek word for *sin* — hamartia — means to miss the center of the target, or miss the mark. Exodus 34:7 uses the words *iniquity*, *transgression*, and *sin*. Three different words for sin? I thought there was only one! Three different words to describe ways I stray from God. Further study reveals *iniquity* is like perversity or moral evil, *transgression* is like rebellion, and in Hebrew the word translated for *sin* can mean a variety of offenses or habitual sins. The good news is also revealed in Exodus 34:7 — His forgiveness covers all three.

When Peter denied Christ, the scriptures say he wept bitterly. Why did he weep? For denying Christ in public? *Oh, Jesus, how often have I done that?* For his pride? For his audacity to contradict the very words of Jesus? *Even if all deny you, I will never!*

Isaiah says, "I am a man of unclean lips, and I live among a people of unclean lips" (Isaiah 6:5 NASB). Unclean language emerged from

Why was Peter weeping bitterly? Matthew 26:75

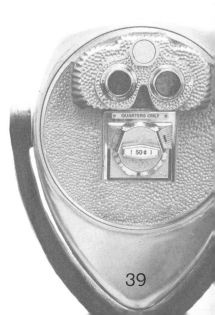

39

Isaiah. Was it gossip, complaining, boasting, slander, making fun of people, lying? All things I've done — oh, how the heart fuels the tongue.

Is my heart sensitive enough to God that when I sin my heart is troubled? Or, like the scar on my thumb, am I unable to feel the things that grieve God?

In Luke 18, Jesus tells of the parable of the two men who went up to the temple to pray. One, a Pharisee, *the bad guy*, and the other a tax collector. Having had a radical conversion at age 16 and having been delivered from deep addictions, I identified with the repentant tax collector, *the good guy*, the guy who couldn't lift his eyes to heaven but in humility prayed "God, be merciful to me, the sinner!" (v. 13 NASB).

As a young believer, a sensitive heart prevailed and tears of repentance frequented my prayer times. Many years passed, and I had lived a "good Christian life." I tithed, went to church, prayed and read scriptures daily, shared the gospel, served others, and had a concern for the poor. But finally something occurred to me — how my prayers over time had subtly become like those of the Pharisee, *the bad guy* in Luke 18 who prayed much like this: *God, I thank you that I am not like thieves, adulterers, swindlers, unjust; I fast twice a week and I tithe.* The only thing that separated me from that Pharisee was that he fasted much more than I did. Oh my, I thought all of those things were good things. Why were they listed on the *bad guy's* list?

What was the difference? A broken, contrite heart. According to Psalm 34:18 (NASB), "The Lord is near to the brokenhearted and saves those who are crushed in spirit." I had become numb to the ways that I offended God. I was still offending God greatly. In fact, I had a huge anger problem apparent to my family and all those who played basketball with me, but I shrugged it off as nothing. My problem: I had forgotten that my sin was ugly to God. I forgot that I still needed the ongoing cleansing of 1 John 1:7. I had quit recognizing and hating my sin. Subtly, slowly, I had become the Pharisee in the parable without even knowing it. My life swelled with spiritual pride, which is still a struggle for me.

I asked God to show me if there was any hurtful way in me, and He graciously showed me the ugliness of sin that permeated my life. Proverbs 8:13 says to fear the Lord is to hate what is evil. I clearly hated the evil in everyone else's life, but I had a numbness and tolerance for my own sin.

Proverbs 15:9 (NASB) says, "The way of the wicked is an abomination to the Lord." *Abomination* is also used in verse 8 to describe the sacrifice of the wicked. The word *abomination*, among other things, means "disgusting." When you think of the word *disgusting,* what comes to mind? When I think of *disgusting* I think of vomit. Also, this thought comes to mind: walking into a public restroom where a full toilet has backed up, spreading feces and urine in the stall. The stench so horrible I want to vomit. Or I think *disgusting* accurately describes the time when my Dad and my brother Jim used hoses to flush out the rat colony from beneath the garage and began stepping on scampering large rats and using an oar to kill them.

Are you offended yet? Am I, are you, repulsed by sin? Or do we tolerate it? We all might agree that human trafficking is disgusting. But what about gossip? Or bitterness? To Jesus, those are also disgusting.

What do you think of when you think of "disgusting"?

In Psalm 51, David said to the Lord, "You desire truth in the innermost being" (v. 6 NASB). Sometimes those hidden parts of me, secret sins, are so ugly I can't even admit I've committed such sins or I refuse to call them sin. Or I've repeated a sin so many times I can't bear to ask forgiveness yet again. Be assured that Jesus practices what He preaches in His words to Peter regarding forgiving someone "seventy times seven" (Matthew 18:22 NASB). He willingly and gladly receives every repentant heart.

When Wendy and I do this exercise, we don't coddle our sin; we confess and begin to hate and forsake it. We list each sin and personally confess it to God. The Greek word for *confess* in 1 John 1:9 is homologeo; it means *to have the same word as.* I am to have the *same word* or agree with God regarding His view of my sin — disgusting.

Sample prayer: Jesus, help me to hate and be sickened by my sin. Forgive me for my sin of spiritual pride. Forgive me for my sin of idolatry when I put money or sports ahead of you. Forgive my sin of gossip or complaining. Jesus, please forgive me for holding bitterness against that person. Forgive me for laughing at perverse TV shows. Forgive me for being so insensitive with my words. Forgive me for always needing to be right. Please forgive me, Jesus, for retelling the faults of others. Please forgive me for a lack of integrity.

Prayer: Show me, Father, right now if there is any hurtful, sinful way in me, any rebellion, or any perversion. Is there anything that offends you in me? Is there something I've been numb to, that you see? Please, Father, reveal it to me. Help me to hate my sin.

RESPONSE

Would you now give Jesus, our Healer and the Great Physician, the freedom to use a spiritual scope to identify any sin blockage in your heart? Write out a list of all sins that come to mind. Then practicing 1 John 1:9, confess the sins, and ask God to forgive you for each sin, trusting Him to forgive you completely.

Now may I encourage you to let God continue His probing by looking at the second common spiritual blockage? Let's go beyond personal sin to corporate sin and let's learn why Ezra was crying.

RECOGNIZE AND CONFESS CORPORATE SIN

Romans 14:12 says each person shall give account of himself to God. **God's Word teaches individual responsibility.** The Bible also teaches that God sees interconnectedness with us as a part of larger groups, like a family, a local church, communities, or even nations. In 1 Corinthians 12, Paul instructs us on how the Body of Christ is one and how it works. Verse 26 says if one member suffers, we all suffer.

In football, one person's bad pass, kick, or poor tackle may cost the entire team a game. In the same way, God's anger may turn toward a family or local church solely based on the sin of one person. Injustice committed by leadership, or some sin that has been allowed or not addressed in our family or organization, may hinder the flow of God's work in our community. This has often been termed *corporate sin.*

There is probably no better example of how one person's sin can impact the entire community than the story of Achan in Joshua 7. Achan clearly disobeyed God by keeping contraband from the victory at Jericho. In doing this evil, God held all of Israel accountable and thwarted their next battle. Once God revealed to Joshua the reason for His displeasure, Joshua dealt with it appropriately as God directed, and God's blessing was restored. Who would have thought that the secret act of one person could take down a whole nation?

Whether the secret sin of a team member or an act of injustice committed by leadership, God takes it seriously. A father's secret sin can poison and hinder an entire family. And parents who do not confront the known sin of their children also are culpable. According to 1 Samuel 2, Eli honored his sons above God by allowing their rampant sinful behavior to continue unchecked. Not only did Eli and his sons Hophni and Phinehas lose their lives for this ugliness, but also Phinehas' wife, who was pregnant at the time, quite appropriately named her fatherless child Ichabod, meaning "God's glory has departed." God's presence may leave or be hindered in our family or our organization when we commit or are complicit in corporate sin, blurring or preventing our ability to see God's vision.

As Ezra confessed, lots of people gathered and wept with him.

Let's look at why Ezra cried (Ezra 10). It's no wonder God so blessed this spiritual leader. Ezra 9 shows us that marriage outside of the faith had become commonplace among the Israelites, a direct violation of God's command (Ezra 9:11, 12). So "while Ezra prayed and made confession, weeping and casting himself down before the house of God, a very great assembly of men, women, and children gathered to him out of Israel, for the people wept bitterly" (Ezra 10:1 ESV). In verse 2, an Israelite, Shecaniah, confesses, "We have broken faith with our God." Yet one man's humility and willingness to take responsibility brought healing to the entire group and pleasure to God.

Have you been complicit in allowing or ignoring a corporate sin?

Is there a known sin that has gone unchecked in your family, organization, or congregation? Has your church or organization treated a former volunteer or staff person inappropriately? Oftentimes God's blessing is withheld until such sin is dealt with properly. Whether or not you personally committed the sin, maybe you can be the one like Ezra to take ownership before God and in confession be the catalyst for healing.

Prayer: God, have we been complicit in allowing or ignoring corporate sin? Is there any secret sin that is holding us back? Is there a person we may have treated unjustly? Is there something close to Your heart that we have omitted, like caring for widows and orphans? Is there a lack of integrity in our organization or church? Are we truthful with our finances? Please, Father, is there anything You want me to do about it?

RESPONSE

Write down any possible corporate sin. Confess it on behalf of your family, group, or organization. As Ezra did, take responsibility for it as if it were your own. Take any action necessary. It may be advisable to seek counsel from a trusted friend before "making a whip and clearing the Temple."

Now let's take a look at the third blockage that may be hindering spiritual circulation — our fears.

RE-VISIONING

Step 4. Honestly identify and admit your fears and take them to Jesus.

I grew up in South Omaha, known as a tough neighborhood, the youngest of six children, one girl and five boys, all successful athletes. I was the "sensitive" kid. I cried at the drop of a hat. But I quickly learned to mask my anxieties and fears with bravado and aggression. Then I met the Lord at age 16. He delivered me from addictions and great ugliness. My boldness and assertiveness turned into a confident, disciplined, fearless faith.

FEAR EXISTS DESPITE OUR FAITH

Somewhere in the transition from wild, unbelieving teen to on-fire believer, I missed something. There were amazing changes in my life, thanks to the grace of God. I received forgiveness, committed myself to study the scriptures, and made disciples. It wasn't until 15 years later, well into my marriage, that God began to reveal to me the deep fear issues gripping my heart. My fears manifested themselves in anger, self-righteousness, and a need to control. These issues were all fear based. God gently used His scope to show me that.

My internal fears caused strange and sinful behavior.

Early in my newfound faith, I had studied 1 John, particularly verse 4:18 where it says **perfect love casts out fear.** At that time, I was taught and believed that verse meant "REAL Christians don't have fear." So I did what I had always done — I masked my fears. But now I did so with a new Christian bravado, even arrogance, that included new "Christian" language and behavior. I showed little compassion for others, especially those with fears, anxiety issues, or weakness of any kind. The problem with masking my fears was that they oozed out in other areas of life, causing strange and sinful behavior.

When I finally learned I could trust God with my fears, fear after fear emptied out of my soul.

When I finally learned I could trust God with the deepest fears of my soul, it was like I had opened a shaken bottle of soda. As soon as the cap was off, fear after fear poured out of my soul. I began to relate all my fears to God: *I am afraid that my children won't get good grades, that they won't make good choices for friends. I'm afraid that they will abandon their faith. I'm afraid I won't be able to meet all my wife's needs. I'm afraid that I won't make enough money to provide for my family. I'm afraid my daughters will never be married; I'm afraid my daughters* will *be married. I'm afraid we won't have enough money to survive or make house payments. I'm afraid to work with this church or organization. I'm intimidated by this leader or this pastor. I fear what people will think of my wife, my children, or me.*

FEAR BRINGS MORE SIN, BUT GOD BRINGS FREEDOM

In 2005 Wendy contracted cancer that required harsh chemotherapy. She lost all her hair. After baldness became reality, Wendy tried hard to get just the right wig to fit, one that wouldn't irritate her scalp and one that matched her natural hair color. She had to purchase several wigs just to manage daily life. They all looked great, very realistic. Yet one was extremely uncomfortable, and another was like wearing an oven.

Let God's provision of forgiveness and deliverance open and cleanse your spiritual arteries.

On one occasion Wendy was leading worship for a conference of 300 leaders of MOPS (Mothers of Preschoolers). I was also doing some training for the same group. On the morning of the second day, before she led worship, Wendy decided she was going to change wigs. I freaked out! "You can't do that," I demanded. "Why?" She responded in disbelief. "Well, because they will all know you are bald. It will draw unnecessary attention to your cancer," I answered. Sadly, I feared what the people might think.

It's hard for me to believe I was so disgusting! Here my wife had demonstrated incredible courage. She was leading worship for the fifth conference in only 12 weeks after major surgery and during her chemo treatments. She was facing cancer recurrence and possible death with great bravery. And MY FEAR, not her fear, was causing me to make a bizarre, controlling, cowardly judgment.

One by one, God helped me to identify and admit my fears to myself and then to my Father, and He greeted each fear not with punishment but with His love. Now for the first time in my life I began to understand 1 John 4:18: "Perfect love casts out fear" (ESV). Our gracious God would happily deliver me from all my fears, but I would have to identify and admit them first to myself and then to God. I learned that so much of my sinful and strange behavior found its impetus in fear. Then God began to deliver me in an amazing way. I experienced a deep spiritual cleansing. As soon as I understood my internal fear and took it to Jesus, my corresponding poor behavior disappeared.

Simultaneous to my newfound freedom, I discovered something amazing in scriptures. I was not alone in my fears. Moses seemed deathly afraid of going alone to Pharaoh. So even though God was angry, He allowed Aaron to go with Moses (Exodus 4:10-17). The great leader Gideon seemed fearful on every front (Judges 6, 7). God asked Gideon to destroy his father's idols. The idols were in the public square and Gideon was fearful to destroy them in the daylight, so God allowed him to do it at night. Gideon feared going down to the camp of the Midianites with only 300 men. Again, God allayed Gideon's fears by having him to witness a supernatural dream on the outskirts of the enemy camp, foretelling his future victory.

Psalm 34:4 says, "I sought the Lord and he answered me and delivered me from all my fears" (ESV). I started to see that David's Psalms are filled with transparency. He expressed his deepest heart feelings in his songs. Fear is not sin, but it can lead to or be the cause of sin.

Could there ever have been a more transparent human heart cry then when Jesus asked the Father if He would be willing to remove the cup? Think about it; why would Jesus sincerely wish "this cup would pass"? Why did He pray this prayer three times? Because He was fully human, even as He was fully God. It's evident through Jesus' prayer (and the Greek words describing the situation in Matthew 26:36-44) that He was deeply disturbed and emotionally distressed on the night before His crucifixion. I am comforted by His humanity.

Paul said in 1 Corinthians 2:3, "I was with you in weakness and in fear and much trembling" (ESV). Paul not only admitted his fear, he talked about it publicly in his letters. "I was with you in weakness [*asthenia* = sickness, frailty] and in fear [*phobos* = fear] and much trembling [*tromos* = shaking with tremors]." The phrase "Do not be afraid" occurs in the Bible numerous times. Some use this to repress fear. However, this phrase tells me how prevalent fear is in the human condition.

"I sought the Lord and He answered me and delivered me from all my fears." – David

1 Peter 5:7 (ESV) says, "Casting all of your anxieties on him."
Why? "Because he cares for you."

Prayer: God, I have so many fears, big and small. There are likely many fears and concerns about my life that I haven't fully identified. Would You help me to identify my deepest fears, and entrust them to You? Show me, Lord, how these fears impact my behavior. Will You deliver me from each and every fear? Show me how to trust You again every time I feel that fear.

God is for me.
Who can be
against me?

RESPONSE

List all your fears and anxieties, small and large. Then one by one, ask God in the name of Jesus to deliver you from that fear. Caution: Simply admit the fear, don't focus on the fear; focus on casting it onto Jesus, entrusting it to Him.

_____

_____

_____

_____

_____

_____

_____

_____

_____

_____

_____

_____

_____

_____

_____

_____

_____

_____

_____

_____

Let's look now at how meditating on God's Word and confessing our sins can restore our spiritual circulation.

RE-VISIONING

Step 5. Experience God's forgiveness and be open to confession.

Meditate on God's forgiveness and deliverance. Become overwhelmed with Jesus' forgiveness, love, and deliverance. *Will you take some time to stop and meditate on the incredible provisions God has given us? Allow yourself to take a long, hot "bath" in the truths of the gospel, and in the provision supplied in the blood of Jesus Christ given to remove blockages from our spiritual life.*

RESPONSE 1 — MEDITATE

Now that you've identified and confessed personal or corporate sins and identified and admitted fears, you've started to allow God to clear blockages that may be hindering your spiritual vision. Now take some time to reflect on God's amazing faithful provision for opening these blockages, available in Jesus. Carefully meditate on the scripture passages and some of your own favorite verses related to God's forgiveness and deliverance. Don't just read through them, but let the truths, like water, run over you.

Read this beautiful passage in Hebrews 4:14-16: "Therefore, since we have a great high priest who has passed through the heavens, Jesus the Son of God, let us hold fast our confession. For we do not have a high priest who cannot sympathize with our weaknesses, but One who has been tempted in all things as we are, yet without sin. Therefore, let us draw near with confidence to the throne of grace, so that we may receive mercy and find grace to help in time of need" (NASB). What better ointment for our sins and fears than God's unlimited provision of mercy and grace awaiting us as we access His forgiveness.

God is for me. Who can be against me? Romans 8:39

Other scriptures about God's forgiveness and deliverance include:
- Romans 8:1: "There is therefore now no condemnation for those who are in Christ Jesus" (ESV).
- Romans 8:31, 38-39: "If God is for us, who can be against us? . . . I am sure that neither death nor life . . . will be able to separate us from the love of God in Christ Jesus our Lord" (ESV).
- Isaiah 6:6-7: After Isaiah's admission of his sin, "One of the seraphim [angels] flew to me with a burning coal in his hand, which he had taken from the altar with tongs. He touched my mouth with it and said, 'Behold, this has touched your lips; and your iniquity is taken away and your sin is forgiven'" (NASB).
- Psalm 103:12: "As far as the east is from the west, so far does he remove our transgressions from us" (ESV).
- Psalm 34:4, 6, 7: "I sought the Lord, and He answered me and

delivered me from all my fears. . . . This poor man cried, and the Lord heard him and saved him out of all his troubles. The angel of the Lord encamps around those who fear Him, and delivers them" (NASB).

- Psalm 34:19: "Many are the afflictions of the righteous, but the Lord delivers him out of them all" (NASB).
- 1 Peter 5:6, 7: "Therefore humble yourselves under the mighty hand of God, that He may exalt you at the proper time, casting all your anxiety on Him, because He cares for you" (NASB).
- 1 John 4:18: "Perfect love casts out fear" (ESV).
- 2 Corinthians 12:7-9: "There was given me a thorn in the flesh. . . . Concerning this I implored the Lord three times that it might leave me. And He said to me, 'My grace is sufficient for you, for power is perfected in weakness'" (NASB).

My sin, your sin, has been paid for! God understands our weakness and wants to deliver us from every fear. Think about God's amazing provision of mercy and grace. And praise Him for it. Thank God for His past deliverance and forgiveness, for all the forgiveness that is ours because of the Cross. Spend time thanking God for the love that is yours in Christ Jesus.

Prayer: Father, thank You for the truths revealed in the gospel of Jesus Christ. Because my sins are paid for by the blood of Jesus, I can confess my sins to You. You not only welcome me, but You rejoice over me when I return to You. You know me; You made me. You know my every thought, my every weakness. You know my frame and my fears. Thank You that Your desire is to deliver and rescue Your child and walk close to me. You will never leave me or forsake me.

RESPONSE 2 — CONSIDER CONFESSION

Would I dare to confess my sin to or share my fears with another?

If you are traveling through this Re-visioning experience by yourself, you may well have to wait for another time to consider the following suggestion. If going through it with your spouse, you may or may not feel comfortable sharing every sin or sidestep with your spouse. Or you may feel it is necessary to share the burden you've identified with another person.

We naturally tend to hide rather than confess our sin, repress rather than admit our fear, pretend rather than acknowledge weakness, and go it alone rather than risk divulging our flaws. These inclinations prevent the Holy Spirit from flowing more freely into our lives and ministries. But now that you've identified and confessed these blockages, I strongly encourage you to consider sharing honestly what you've identified with one other person.

By God's amazing grace for the last two decades I have rarely been sick or, if I have, the illness has been short lived. However, in 2010, I contracted a strange virus that would not go away. Finally I sought medical care. Two rounds of antibiotics later, nothing had changed. I begged God repeatedly for healing and yet nothing changed. Weeks later, the ailment remained. Though I finally made it to church, the fever started raging again during the service. During an altar call for prayer, I unloaded the burden on our associate pastor and he prayed for me. THAT WAS IT!! From that moment forward, my sickness was gone. God doesn't always heal like that. In fact, God doesn't always choose to heal us. But I am convinced that God wanted me to humble myself and share my burden with someone else before He would heal me.

My former pastor said, "Together is God's design." No man, no woman, is an island. I've learned just how much God wants me to understand that I am a part of the Body of Christ and I can't function alone. My weaknesses are the strengths of others. Their weaknesses may be my strength.

God might not release you from a stronghold until you share it with someone else.

55

May I give you four good reasons to divulge your weaknesses, sins, and fears to one another?

1. Scripture tells us to do so: James 5:16 says confess your faults one to another that you may be healed.
The Greek word for *faults* means "sidesteps." In 2 Corinthians 12:9, Paul not only is willing to share he has weaknesses with the entire church at Corinth, but says, "Therefore, I will boast all the more gladly of my weaknesses, so that the power of Christ may rest upon me" (ESV). And I love the transparency of the Psalms. The man after God's own heart, David, seems to reveal his every gut-wrenching feeling. In Psalm 51, David confesses his sin and verse 10 says, "Create in me a clean heart, O God, and renew a right spirit within me" (ESV). In fact, according to the Psalm's introduction, it was written as a song for the congregation to sing regularly.

2. Confession, humbling ourselves to one another, guards us against self-righteousness.
Admitting my weakness to others reminds me and reveals to others that I am not perfect. I am in process. That perspective keeps marriages and families and churches at the foot of the Cross. So many pastors and Christian leaders struggle in isolation because they feel they can't trust others with information as they fear they would lose respect. Yet that isolation drives many deeper into secret sin. They remain isolated and elevated from their teams or congregations, making matters worse.

3. Confession shows us the nature of God's plan — *together is His design* — not independence.
God desires the Church to work much like the human body. The body exhibits a tremendous interdependence. Paul says to the Ephesians, "We are to grow up in all aspects into Him who is the head, even Christ, from whom the whole body, being fitted and held together by what every joint supplies, according to the proper working of each individual part" (Ephesians 4:15, 16 NASB).

4. God might not release you from a stronghold until you admit it to another person.

The evil one's power is magnified in our secret sins and fears. His ability to manipulate and pour guilt and condemnation on us allow him to control us with accusation, guilt, and fear, but admitting our weakness to another punctures the evil one's ability to control and use it against us.

Prayer: Lord, if you want me to share with another what I have been holding inside in order to deliver me, please give me the courage to do it. Show me the appropriate person and give me the courage not to delay.

RESPONSE 3 — CONFESS TO ONE ANOTHER

Once you have completed reviewing the sections on sins, corporate sin, and fears, I strongly encourage you to consider doing two things:

1. **Get with one partner of the same gender who can be trusted with great confidentiality and share as much as you can.**

2. **Spend time listening and praying for each other.**

In Isaiah 6, after admitting his sins and experiencing forgiveness, Isaiah says, "Then I heard the voice of the Lord" (NASB). God's clear voice came directly after Isaiah's confession and experience of cleansing.

"Then I heard the voice of the Lord."
Isaiah 6:8 (NASB)

Likewise in Luke 5, Peter, amazed at the supernatural catch of fish, and realizing his humble state before God, falls at Jesus' feet saying, "Go away from me Lord, for am a sinful man!" (v. 8 NASB). In verse 10, Jesus reveals Peter's mission: "Do not fear, from now on you will be catching men." At the precise time that Peter is broken and at Jesus' feet, and begging Jesus to go away, Jesus confounds Peter. It's as if Jesus were saying, "Okay, now I've got you exactly where I want you — humble, aware of your sinfulness, and completely vulnerable and dependent on me. Now I can use you; go and serve."

God's power is perfected and revealed in weakness! He doesn't build His kingdom with confident, able, intellectual people; rather He uses the rejected "stuff" and supernaturally empowers it with His might.

God uses broken people who are equal at the foot of the Cross.

PAY ATTENTION TO WHAT GOD IS SAYING AND WHERE HE IS LEADING

If you've completed the previous sections on removing blockages, be ready to hear what God might be saying. This next part of Re-visioning is paying attention to God's voice and direction for you.

RE-VISIONING

Step 6. To what do you *know* God has called you?

....

This question deserves analysis. Many times as I've removed spiritual blockages and wiped clean my spiritual lenses, God reveals to me what I've been missing!

A window seat on an airplane and the view from the top of a hill offer unique perspective. As a ministry consultant to Christian leaders for many years, God has given our ministry a unique perspective, a view of His Body that few get to see. We get to work with many large, worldwide Christian organizations and with many local and large churches. Perhaps one of the greatest mistakes we've seen is that they veer off the specific call God has given them and attempt to take on responsibility for every local and global need.

While on staff as National Director of Volunteers at Compassion International, I visited a Christian organization in England called Tearfund. Among other things, Tearfund serves the poor greatly by offering products to Christians that are made by poor people in less-developed countries. I was so excited by their effective microenterprise operation that when I returned I tried to persuade Wally Erickson, then president of Compassion, to consider adding such a ministry so that Compassion could meet more needs. I'm not sure I'll ever forget his response. After applauding Tearfund for their ministry, Wally said, "Al, God has called us to do Christian child development — we do that well. There will always be unlimited need and yet every organization possesses only a limited amount of resources. We must focus our limited resources exactly as God has called us to make the greatest impact."

Is your life or ministry a wide-spray or narrow-spray nozzle?

A focused life and a streamlined ministry make leading and following a whole lot easier. It's when we get off track that we encounter greater distractions.

Imagine there are five rocks of equal size in front of you and that your assignment is to move one rock 10 feet using a hose. Using the "narrow" spray, you immediately focus the hose on one rock and it begins to move forward. However, the presence of the other four rocks grabs your attention. You turn the nozzle to "wide-spray" position in order to reach all the rocks. Though you are now able to reach every rock, the water pressure is so weak that you are able to only dampen each rock and unable to *move* any rock. This represents one of the greatest problems in churches today. The many needs in our peripheral vision turn our focus from God's specific calling, weakening the power and stream of energy and focus needed to bear great fruit and making us ineffectual.

Jim Harrelson, vice president of Samaritan's Purse Operation Christmas Child and one of the greatest leaders you've never heard of, spends every bit of energy on leveraging every resource to advance the gospel. His life is focused on getting the gospel to

children and offering them the opportunity to experience discipleship. It's no wonder the ministry under his leadership has grown from thousands of shoebox gifts to more than 10 million gifts delivered to children with gospel and discipleship intent every year! I wonder what would have happened had Jim not maintained such an ardent focus.

Don't forget the very reason you went to the grocery store.

So often, missing the specific calling of God, like the wide-spray nozzle, diffuses our ability to make a real difference and makes it difficult for staff and volunteers to follow. Could it be that you have veered off your "mission"?

COMMON MISTAKES LEADERS MAKE THAT GET THEM "OFF VISION"

1. They forget the Great Commission and the Great Commandment in their picture of the future.
It's like going to the store to get bananas. On my way, I realize we need paper towels, coffee, ice cream, and milk. I get the paper towels, coffee, ice cream and milk, and it's not until I get home that I realize I've forgotten the bananas, the very reason I left the house.

The Great Commission and the Great Commandment should remain the reason we *leave the house*. Every Christ-focused organization and leader is called to complete the Great Commission — to make disciples of all nations — and to apply the "royal commandment" of scripture — to love your neighbor. These two mandates should always reside near the top of our "grocery list." They must be central to our church or organization's specific reasons for existence.

2. They don't make their spouse and children a priority.
Every husband has been called to love and honor his wife. Wives are called to love and honor their husbands. Be assured that God does not plan on wrecking your marriage in order to plant a church or grow your organization. The scripture teaches that husband and wife are one. God's vision can most often be detected when there is strong agreement between husband and wife. Wendy's discernment has

saved us from making many poor life decisions. At the same time, I've witnessed that one spouse can be so strong that the other reluctantly complies in many situations. That often spells disaster when it comes to vision.

Similarly, parents are called to love and nurture their children. Rest assured that our loving heavenly Father will not call you to abandon your children in order to accomplish His will. This does not mean, however, that there won't be sacrifices that families have to make.

When the scriptures say that we are the Bride of Christ, we can know that Jesus is not an absent spouse off to conquer something more important. When the Bible says God is our Father, He is not abandoning us for some greater cause. He is our present Dad. He pays attention to us and abides with us. No ministry or Christian leader will be as effective as he or she can be if the more fundamental callings of being a spouse or parent are abandoned.

3. They quickly abandon God's previously revealed specific vision. Though God's specific calling to volunteer ministry development was clear to Wendy and me, we couldn't see how we would be able to make it work financially with only a Christian focus. So our first messaging attempts were directed at a broader audience to include all not-for-profits. Within a month God showed us our mistake, when thankfully only Christian organizations replied to our marketing. *What was I thinking?* Our message is biblically based and Christ centered; our ministry is simply not aligned with those other types of organizations. In our second year, seeing how powerful High Impact volunteers were in the marketing arena, we entertained sharing marketing advice as a service, then quickly abandoned that as it just didn't fit. Others asked us to do leadership training. Many now come asking us for advice on being consultants. All of those are worthy endeavors, but not for us. Our calling is *to walk alongside Christian leaders as they develop deep-rooted, high-impact volunteer ministries to the worldwide Body of Christ.*

Jesus is not an absent spouse. Our loving Father does not call us to abandon our children.

In my experience, leaders know the specific calling God has given, but often neglect it for yet another worthy idea. The Body of Christ is enormous and beautifully crafted. As great as your organization or church is, it remains a small part of the Body. We must trust that God has a plan for the needs we see outside of our calling. John 6 reports that after experiencing Jesus' miracle of feeding thousands, the people intended to make Jesus their king by force. Of course, Jesus could have become king, but He remained focused on the Cross, the purpose for which He came.

Don't let the sensuality of something new get you off vision.

In Revelation 3:2, Jesus reminds the church at Sardis that their "work" is not complete in the sight of God. Don't let the sensuality of something new distract you from the mission for which God has designed you.

Prayer: You know how You have designed me. I want to be faithful to Your calling, Your specific mission. Please, I want to have a clear focus on what You want me to do. If You've already shown me and I've neglected this, please remind me, make it fresh. Or please show me now.

RESPONSE

Take some time to list from your past experiences with God and from the illumination of His Word what you know for sure you are called to do. For instance, *I know I am called to get to know God better each day. I know I am called to love my spouse and my children. I know God has revealed to our church that we are to reach 20 somethings or 70 somethings. I know God has called me to minister in India* [or some other specific location]. You may include in this what you know about your individual gifting. For example, I *know God has gifted me in leadership* [or in worship ministry, or with children].

_____

_____

_____

_____

_____

_____

_____

_____

_____

_____

_____

_____

_____

_____

_____

_____

_____

_____

_____

_____

_____

_____

_____

Another key way to streamline your ministry focus is by identifying those areas in your life that are fruit producing.

Step 7. Where do you see spiritual fruit in your life and ministry?

You may believe you have a gift for teaching adults or children. However, if each week the number of students in your class dwindles, you may want to reconsider that notion. Doing an honest "fruit inspection" of our life and ministry can be a great way to help us identify wasted effort and energy so that we can refocus our resources on the ministry and life activities we were designed to do and hence assigned to complete. This process often makes our lives simpler and more productive.

A woman with a great gift of administration loved to sing in our church services. She may have felt *called* to sing. To say she had major pitch problems grossly understates the situation. I hate to admit it, but before inviting visitors, I would check to make sure she was *not* singing. She not only was deaf to her own vocal limitations, but also was unable to hear the beautiful "music" produced by her administrative gifts.

In John 15:8, Jesus said, "My Father is glorified by this, that you bear much fruit" (NASB). In verse 16 He adds, "I . . . appointed you that you would go and bear fruit, and that your fruit would remain." Healthy trees produce fruit. Be confident that if God has called you, eventually fruit will result. This does not mean your church plant will exceed 1,000 people in the first year, or that each time you teach you should expect crowds to increase. In fact, numbers may have nothing to do with fruit at all. It may be a mentoring relationship that is flourishing or the internal fruit of the Spirit growing as a result of an accountability group. Or maybe you are seeing fruit in your new approach to Bible study. Maybe you see that your extended family is healthier because of a weekly Sunday meal you offer.

In what ministry activities do you see God's power unleashed?

In what activities do you see God's power unleashed? Do you experience great joy in those? Do others confirm your giftedness?

Our prayer team's ability to access God and bring forth His power in our ministry is dynamic. We always have a section in our courses focused on prayer and the importance of developing prayer teams. Ruth, one of our prayer partners, formerly worked as an assistant for the National Day of Prayer. Ruth became one of our High Impact volunteer prayer team members. Seeing her passion for prayer and the effectiveness of her prayer, we invited Ruth to participate at our courses. In her sixties and into her seventies, Ruth shared at every event. Ruth did not possess a polished speaking style, nor did she use PowerPoint or any object lessons. She never employed the many techniques that our training sessions are known for, yet frequently

her talk was noted as the most impacting moment of our event. Countless hundreds of prayer groups have been started because of Ruth's talks. God's power was activated through this amazing volunteer.

Eric Liddell, Scottish Olympic champion and missionary to China, was the key subject of the Oscar-winning Best Picture of 1981, *Chariots of Fire.* A scene portrays Liddell's thoughts as he is about to win a hard-fought race: *When I run, I feel His pleasure.* In what areas or activities of your life do you sense God's pleasure? His power?

Prayer: Lord, bring to my mind those big areas and simple areas in my life where You are working, where You are producing health, growth, or fruit. Help me to be objective, not just about those things I like to do, but also about those that are aligned with Your plan for me. Let me identify those tasks I love to do and that are producing fruit — even the ones that require hard work and sacrifice.

RESPONSE

Take a few minutes to make a list of the fruit-producing areas in your personal life and in your organization. Ask yourself, *Where do I see fruit in my personal life? Family life? What areas of our church or organization are producing great, lasting fruit? Where do I see God's supernatural power unleashed? What ministry efforts seem to be blessed by growth or fruit?* For example, you might list, "These two people I'm discipling." Or you might list, "When I serve at the rescue ministry, when I organize things or when I cook meals and show hospitality, when I serve children, when I speak or teach, or when I exercise." Also list the areas in your church or organization that are producing great fruit: "Our ministry to children produces fruit" or "Our tutoring ministry, our worship ministry, or our volunteer advocate ministry."

_____

_____

_____

_____

_____

_____

_____

_____

_____

_____

_____

_____

_____

_____

_____

_____

_____

You've spent some time identifying those areas you know God has called you and/or your organization to, and you've also focused on areas where fruit is being produced in your life and ministry.

In the next step of Re-visioning, we take some moments to locate those areas that may be hindering fruit production or that will hinder production if we don't act soon.

Step 8. What keeps you from being fruitful or healthy?

What keeps a tree from being fruitful? There are both internal and external factors. Internally, the tree might suffer from poor soil or a lack of water or sunlight. Externally, bug infestations or the onslaught of hail could damage fruit. Similarly, the growth of ministry fruit can be hindered by both internal and external factors. What risks exist both personally and organizationally that might keep your ministry from being fruitful?

When a prospective client approaches, we seek God as to whether or not we should engage them. As best we could tell earlier in our ministry, God gave the green light to beginning relationships with one new client after another. The intensity of our lives and ministry had been far beyond human capacity, and yet now was multiplying out of control. The sense of "overwhelming" did not create a situation where we were simply inviting more of God's power to fill the gap, but one where we could not keep up. For the first time in our ministry, we could not keep up with the details. Assignments were late; we were asking for forgiveness more and more. Not only that, clients were asking more of us, and it seemed they were taking advantage of us.

Then a major new client approached us, a ministry partner that would allow us further global impact. The prospect of working with that organization captivated my heart, and yet our exhaustion was so great. They requested that we start immediately. But how could we? We were already over capacity. That's when Kent, a good friend and prayer partner, who had been sensing our deep dilemma through our prayer notes, gave some simple advice: "Al, I'm sure God would want you to be healthy and able to serve your clients well." Though he says he didn't mean it that way, I took it as admonishment.

All of a sudden, I could see with clarity. My exhaustion, coupled with the growing demands of clients, was blinding my ability to see God's better choices for me. Being faithful to the small things with clients had always been a closely held value of our ministry. I might have thought God was giving me green lights to take on clients, but the reality of being late with assignments and diminishing health punched a hole in that thinking.

Also during this period, another long-term friend, Dave, sharing Kent's same concern for our health and the health of our ministry, encouraged us to take longer breaks, longer vacations. I so loved that idea, partly because it takes me two complete days to wind

My exhaustion was blinding my ability to see God's best choices.

down before I can even appreciate a vacation. Wendy and I have always done well making sure to spend time with each other and taking time to get away. We would frequently tag on two or three days or take a multi-day vacation after events. Yet, the increased volume of ministry required a change as the work began encroaching even on our free time.

The loving admonishment from both prayer partners (also Christian leaders) resulted in several changes:

1. We did take on the new major client, but I asked if we could delay the start of the contract. Oddly, though under enormous pressure, they agreed.

2. We soon took a long vacation.

3. In addition to seeking God's guidance, we added further criteria to our analysis of whether to engage a new client.

How thankful we were to Kent and Dave for their love and concern to speak up. The adjustments we made have ensured a healthier environment and a better approach to life and ministry.

Prayer: You are a good Father and You love Your children. You are for me. Help me to see myself as You see me. Reveal to me what areas in my life are unhealthy or that I have been neglecting. Please reveal to me those things that need changing for me to be healthier. Show me if there are any serious danger points before it's too late.

RESPONSE

Take some time now to identify existing personal or ministry risks that would either prevent you from being fruitful or that may be hindering more ministry productivity.

LISTEN TO GOD

Now we turn to a crucial part of Re-visioning — as we look to the Word of God.

RE-VISIONING

Step 9. Hear God's voice through scripture.

In Isaiah 6 we read the prophet's experience with God was like a roller coaster of emotion, softening his heart. Isaiah was lifted high in God's temple, overwhelmed with the beauty and greatness of God, then humbly confessed his sin and the sin of his people. He saw that before God, he was nothing. Then the angel touched his lips with a burning coal, signifying God's great mercy and forgiveness. I can only imagine the peace Isaiah must have felt as he experienced the freedom of forgiveness. Then Isaiah says, "Then I heard the voice of the Lord" (Isaiah 6:8 NASB).

LISTEN TO THE STILL, SMALL VOICE

Years ago, I sat in a gym full of screaming kids and parents during a boys and girls basketball tournament, waiting to coach my son and his team in an upcoming game. The girls' game going on in front of me captured my interest. That's when I noticed a man sitting quietly a few bleacher rows in front of me. He sat so still I concluded he had no interest in the game at hand. Then a whistle blew and the referee called a foul on the far end of the court. That's when this man suddenly rose to his feet. Cupping his hands over his mouth, he said in a voice barely above a whisper, "Kristin, Kristin."

Being the intense person that I am, I thought, *You idiot, she's never going to hear you.* But the girl who was fouled turned her head toward the man in the stands and gave her full attention. The man, obviously her dad, aligned his hands as if he were shooting a free throw and, while demonstrating the proper shooting technique, said, "Kristin, follow-through, follow-through." Kristin stood calmly at the free-throw line as the referee handed her the ball. She dribbled twice, and then with perfect form and terrific follow-through sank both free throws!

That's when a light went on in my head. *Wouldn't it be great,* I thought, *if through all the noise, I gave complete attention and focus to the whisper of my heavenly Father's still small voice. Wouldn't it be great if my heart were so sensitive that when my heavenly Father called my name, every part of my body, soul, and mind would focus on His words.*

Isaiah 6 continues: "Then I heard the voice of the Lord, saying, 'Whom shall I send, and who will go for Us?' Then Isaiah said, "Here I am. Send me!" (v. 8 NASB).

HEAR GOD THROUGH SCRIPTURE

There may be many ways God speaks to His people, but who can deny the potency of the very Word of God, the Bible.

Psalm 119 shows the multi-faceted beauty of God's Word to direct our journey.

- Psalm 119:105: The Word of God is a lamp to our feet and a light to our path. The entirety of Psalm 119 reinforces the power and characteristics of God's Word.
- Psalm 19: The Word of God restores the soul, makes us wise, enlightens our eyes, and even warns us. God's vision, His picture of the future to which He is calling us, the compelling spiritual sight, is enlivened by the powerful Word of God.
- 2 Timothy 3:16: All scripture is God-breathed and profitable for teaching, correction, and guiding the man of God in righteousness.
- Nehemiah 9: During a day of spiritual renewal, the Israelites spent a fourth of the day not only confessing their sins and worshipping, but also spent a fourth of the day reading from God's Word. The priority of God's Word in the life of His people remains central.

During a Re-visioning–type day, the Israelites spent a fourth of the day reading from God's Word. Nehemiah 9:3

I can't imagine cutting down a tree without some kind of a saw. A saw remains the perfect tool for that function. So the scriptures are the ideal tool to find or confirm God's direction or vision. Moving without sonar would spell disaster for a submarine. Likewise, a Christian leader or a team trying to move forward without the advice, confirmation, or correction of God's Word is unwise. In this critical part of Re-visioning, we want to spend some focused time seeking God in His Word.

I hope by this point in your journey through this Re-visioning exercise that God has touched you. The stain of the world sticks to our lives the same way some odors stick to our clothes. I hope the salve of the Lord Jesus has begun to melt away some of the hardness that can develop in Christians over time.

Prayer: God, please speak to me. Please show me passages in Your Word that will direct me or confirm for me the direction You have for me.

RESPONSE

Having resensitized our hearts through fasting, prayer, repentance, and honest communication, let us now ask God for clear direction or vision. Tell God, as Isaiah did, "Here I am . . . I am open to what you have for me." Ask Him to divinely lead you to Bible passages that will shed light on your life and ministry and the future picture that He has for you, your church, or organization. He may remind you of and direct you toward passages you already know. Perhaps through this Re-visioning process the Holy Spirit has already given you scriptures to think about. He may direct you or team members to entirely new scriptures. It's very important right now to listen, to be still, to allow God to speak to your soul. It's crucial not to let feelings overtake what God might be saying. Spend 30 to 60 minutes seeking God in this way.

List the scriptures God has given along with any insights you have gained.

Use your
God-given
mental faculties
to test what you
are hearing.

_____

_____

_____

_____

_____

_____

_____

_____

_____

_____

_____

_____

_____

_____

_____

_____

_____

_____

Wendy and I have discovered something remarkable as we have practiced this exercise as a couple and with our team. Once our team comes back together, remarkably similar themes emerge. Sometimes God has revealed to us separately the same verses or passages, or scriptures with identical themes. On one occasion Wendy and I returned and shared key verses. I shared a verse from the New Testament and God had directed her to the same verse in the Old Testament. During one prayer and fasting day, two of our team members were given the same Psalm and almost every team member received verses dealing with the theme of spiritual warfare, specifically dealing with enemies.

DECIDE WHAT TO DO GOING FORWARD

It's important whether you are completing Re-visioning by yourself or with a team that you now use your God-given mental faculties to "test the spirits to see whether they are from God" as 1 John 4:1 (NASB) instructs us. Or as Paul says in 1 Thessalonians 5:21, "examine everything carefully; hold fast to that which is good" (NASB).

Many strategic plans begin by mistakenly asking what needs people see around them, but *God's vision* must start with illumination of His will to our minds. Jesus said, "Blessed are the pure in heart for they shall see God" (Matthew 5:8 ESV). The Greek word for *see* means to gaze upon God as if seeing something remarkable. Remember, even Jesus did nothing on His own initiative. I trust by now that clear direction is emerging.

After a concentrated time in God's Word, and using the entire Re-visioning experience as a foundation, review and complete the final four steps.

"Examine everything carefully." – Paul

Step 10. What would you do if you didn't fear anything?

If I didn't fear anything, I would . . .

_____

_____

_____

_____

_____

_____

_____

Wow, the freedom in answering that question. Oh, the clarity in contemplating *NO limits*. Once our heart is clear, the answer to that question alone can be a strong factor, even the crystalizing agent, in distinguishing God's direction.

In our trainings, I often have people take this quick two-question Bible quiz:

Question 1. Name the two spies.

Since most are Christian leaders, many easily cite Joshua and Caleb.

Question 2. Name the 10 spies.

I have yet to meet anyone who could name one of the other 10 men. Yet these 10 had an enormous impact on God's Nation.

In Numbers 13, the vision of God was crushed in the hearts of 10 of the 12 spies sent out to assess the Promised Land. A lens of fear blinded them, causing them to translate the obstacles as impassable. Their lack of faith caused them to give a poor report of the land, even though they agreed it was a good land (Numbers 13:31, 32). Their lack of faith blinded the entire nation and brought a severe discipline on the entire congregation — having to wait 40 years before they would have the opportunity to enter the Land. However, Joshua and Caleb used a lens of faith to interpret the same circumstances. Numbers 13:30 reports Caleb quieted the people saying, "Let us go up at once and occupy it, for we are well able to overcome it" (ESV).

Don't let fear cause you to miss God's amazing adventure.

Joshua and Caleb used a lens of faith to interpret circumstances.

Reducing alternative routes makes the focus of our journey very clear.

I would but . . . we don't have the money. I can't because I have to work. That can never happen because we can't afford the equipment. What will my family think of me? What will others think of me? We've never done it that way. We don't have the time or human resources. Many of these reasons have cut off God's vision in my own heart. Here's what Joshua and Caleb understood: It is our job to try to understand God's will and act on it. It's His job to provide the power and the resources to overcome the obstacles.

This is a not a license for stupidity or putting God to a foolish test. Don't recklessly consider things that are inconsistent with God's Word. On the other hand, don't let fear cause you to miss God's amazing adventure. Imagine if Noah had said no to building the ark? God's vision often requires steps of faith before we are able to see the provision of resources. Consider Joshua 3: The waters parted *as* the priests carried the Ark of the Lord into the Jordan River.

RESPONSE

Now list all things you would do in your life and ministry if you did not fear a thing. For instance,

- I would start this new ministry.
- I would confront this situation.
- We would move to a new place so that God could use us more.
- I would volunteer for this ministry.
- I would ask for forgiveness for . . .
- I would go on this mission trip.
- We would take the next step of . . .

RE-VISIONING

Step 11. What do you know without a doubt you should *continue* to do?

Many attending our courses have asked how we have retained our passion for our ministry for such a long time. Re-visioning has been key, as it has *reduced our possible options*. We are not stressed by the distraction of alternative ministry choices. We are not contemplating becoming a marketing ministry or consultant for secular organizations. We are confident of our direction and therefore able to head down the path with great conviction. Proverbs 16:9 says, "The mind of a man plans his way, but the Lord directs his steps" (NASB). At this stage of Re-visioning we hope that God has reduced your choices and made clear at least some things you know without a doubt you should continue to do.

Prayer: Let me hear You with clarity, God. What is it that I should definitely keep doing?

RESPONSE

Now list out the things you know without a doubt you should continue to do in your life and ministry. For instance,

- I must continue my times each morning with the Lord.
- I must continue leading that Bible study.
- I need to keep our "date night" a priority.
- I must continue giving to the mission in Africa.
- I need to continue developing the training for our life group leaders.
- I need to keep having breakfast once a week with my friends.
- I need to keep exercising regularly.
- We need to keep our vacations a priority.
- I need to keep our team meetings a priority.

RE-VISIONING

Step 12. What do you need to *stop doing*?

··

When it comes to vision, maybe as important as what *to do* is having a clear vision on what *to stop doing*.

In 1992, the Lord's call on our lives was perfectly clear. Our vision was and is to walk alongside Christian leaders as they develop deep-rooted, high-impact volunteer ministries to the worldwide Body of Christ. In order to move that vision forward, in late 2000, we created *The High Impact Ministry Report (HIMR)*, a monthly periodical to serve Christian leaders. After a few years, we had more than 200 happy subscribers. Wendy and I felt immense satisfaction each month as we sent it to our constituents. However, our energies and resources were significantly consumed by HIMR. We had to ask ourselves, *Is this best use of God's resources to accomplish the vision He has given us?* In late 2003, after completing this Re-visioning exercise, it became clear we were going to have to KILL the HIMR! And in early 2004, by faith we KILLED IT!

As tough as the choice was, the moment we made the decision we were elated. It's funny; prior to the decision we couldn't fully imagine the joy and freedom that was to come. Yet once it was finalized, a huge load lifted. Not only that, we immediately sensed we had made absolutely the right decision. *Why didn't we do this sooner?* Something again we couldn't fully understand until the choice was made. That decision proved a watershed moment in our lives and ministry. Within days, two large ministries requested us to partner with them. One of those ministries was Samaritan's Purse Operation Christmas Child. That turned into a global ministry partnership that has lasted well over a decade.

Are there some very good endeavors, maybe even great ones, that have captured your strength and resources yet may need to be terminated so your energies may be more focused on God's clear vision?

WHAT ABOUT RELATIONSHIPS?

Imagine giving up a relationship, one that you have had for years. What if it meant cutting off someone you love dearly? What if that relationship involved your parent, sibling, or child? Consider what Abraham had to do. Hagar was Sarah's bondservant. Desperate to provide a child for her aging husband, Abraham, Sarah offered Hagar as a substitute. Hagar conceived and gave birth to Ishmael, Abraham's first son. Genesis 16:4 shows that pride swelled in Hagar, as she began to look down on Sarah.

Genesis 21:9-21 reveals that 14 years later this division not only existed, but also was exacerbated by Ishmael's mocking of Sarah's family — making coexistence impossible. When Sarah could bear it no longer, she demanded that Abraham cast out Hagar and Ishmael. Though Abraham was torn, he made the difficult decision. He honored his wife above his child and ultimately trusted God for the future of both Hagar and Ishmael.

89

Talk about tough decisions, Abraham let Ishmael go. Genesis 21:14

Cutting away the excess, or letting go of an idea, may increase the flow of God's Spirit.

I've known many people whose lives are thwarted as they remain in toxic or abusive relationships for which there is no solution. Perhaps one of the most costly mistakes we've observed in our work across the Body of Christ is leadership's lack of will when it comes to terminating a clearly ineffective, even cancerous team member. I must also point out, however, that reconciliation is highly important and must be pursued first. We must respect people as people and not as commodities. Decisions to continue or end relationships must be made carefully while we prayerfully seek God's wisdom.

Life is full of difficult decisions. Remaining in the center of God's will may mean ending a relationship or terminating a sin or behavior. Cutting away the excess, saying no to certain endeavors, or letting go of an idea may enable the flow of God's Spirit and make clear His next assignment.

Prayer: Lord, show me clearly what I need to stop doing. Show me what or who I need to "let go of" to make room for Your best.

RESPONSE

List any practices, sins, relationships, ideas, or endeavors that you are convinced you need to end. For instance,

- I need to quit rehearsing negative thoughts about things I can't control.
- I need to stop listening to gossip.
- I need to let go of my dream of being a famous singer.
- We need to end or change a relationship.
- I need to terminate that part of our ministry that is not producing any fruit.
- I need to dismiss that volunteer.
- We need to stop going deeper into debt.
- I need to stop condemning myself for past sin that Jesus has paid for.
- I need to stop watching inappropriate movies or TV shows.

_____

_____

_____

_____

_____

_____

_____

_____

_____

_____

_____

_____

_____

Now let's turn to the next and last step
of the Re-visioning process.

RE-VISIONING

Step 13. What do you need to *start doing?*

....

After a day of prayer and fasting in 1995, Wendy felt certain our ministry needed to establish a formal prayer team. Prior to that, my grandmother and my mom invoked God's power and presence into our ministry through their relentless appeals to the Father. However, my grandmother went to be with Jesus in September 1993, and in October 1994, we lost my mother. A noticeable "power outage" resulted. Establishing that prayer team has proven to be the most strategic decision our ministry has ever made. Are you convinced you need to begin any major life or ministry strategies? What are they?

I need to golf more. I need to watch more football guilt free. Those two items represent real items on my previous "start doing" lists. Not all matters on this list need to represent earth-shattering decisions. Many may be simple notions that have a big impact. Previously during the process of Re-visioning, God revealed to me that I can possess an unhealthy balance. My too-focused ministry approach made me . . . well, "un-fun." With encouragement from Wendy and other family members, I picked up golf again. The exercise, the mental break from ministry, and the beauty of the golf course were just what I needed.

I need to watch more football guilt free.

What this realization instilled in me was the discipline of carving rest into my schedule, loving myself enough to rest. This practice has had and continues to have a powerful impact on my life, and therefore influences the flow of ministry output as well. As you consider what God would have you do, list those items that have come as a result of today's time of nearness with the Lord as you have sought Him.

Prayer: Lord, there is so much I'm feeling right now. But please let the conviction of the Spirit, not my feelings, rule as I make this list. Please allow only that which is from You to end up on this list.

RESPONSE

Make a list of all strategies and activities, both major initiatives and what may seem like minor ideas, that you are convinced you need to start doing. For instance,

- We need to start a prayer team.
- We need to reinstate the prison ministry.
- We need to invite our neighbors to dinner.
- I need to begin to be faithful about my Bible reading plan.
- I need to schedule a vacation.
- I need to visit my family.
- I need to start school.
- I need to eat better, exercise more.
- I need to purchase a new computer.

RE-VISIONING

Act Now!

There may be something you missed doing in the past, but the past is the past. Make the next right decision and act now. Scripture provides powerful examples of God's people moving into action and here are but a few of them:

After hearing God's voice, Noah began gathering resources and building the ark. Exodus 35 reports that Moses, after hearing God's clear vision, began to recruit resources and volunteers to build the Tabernacle.

I love the urgency and resolve of King Hezekiah. Second Chronicles 29:3 **reports that, at 25 years old, "in the first year of his reign, in the first month,** he opened the doors of the house of the Lord and repaired them." That step initiated powerful reforms and a spiritual revival for the whole of Judah. "And every work that he [Hezekiah] undertook in the service of the house of God and in accordance with the law and the commandments, seeking his God, he did with all his heart, and prospered" (2 Chronicles 31:21 ESV).

In Joshua 18:3, "Joshua said to the people of Israel, 'How long will you put off going in to take possession of the land, which the Lord, the God of your fathers, has given you?'" (ESV). God had "given" the land to His people. It was their responsibility to walk by faith and take it! This passage demonstrates unequivocally that our lack of response, our lack of urgency, can impact the completion or timing of God's vision. The failure of the 10 spies and their derogatory influence on the nation of Israel delayed the Hebrews' entrance into the Promised Land for 40 years.

Years ago, I had lunch with Paul, a faithful donor to our personal support when we served with Youth for Christ. I shared how I believed God was directing me to go to seminary. I was 24 at the time. Without flinching, Paul said he also had felt strongly about going to seminary for years. I could see the conviction in his spirit, and yet at this point in his life it seemed too late, for Paul was 55. For decades, Paul had possessed a conviction to attend seminary and yet had done nothing about it. What made the moment stranger was that Paul talked as if it were still going to happen. At that moment, God used Paul's lack of urgency as a warning to me. "Al, If you don't act now, you'll be sitting here decades from now, talking about it. Do it!" So Wendy and I acted. The schooling was great, but the move to Denver proved to be the force that radically changed and enhanced our lives.

After hearing God's voice, Noah started working.

97

If I can impress one concept on you, it's this: **Your Re-visioning experience will be worthless unless you act.**

Once in a high-school study period, one teacher — a coach whom I respected — wrote on the board,

One action is worth 20 intentions. — Anonymous

One action
is worth
20 intentions.

1. START NOW! If there is anything that you can do right now, do it! For example, make a checklist for yourself:
   - ☐ Did my first reading for my "Read the Bible in a Year" plan today.
   - ☐ I started affirming my spouse more today.
   - ☐ I didn't gossip this evening.

2. Review everything you have done today at the earliest possible time and no later than tomorrow. Wendy and I often review the scriptures the Lord gave us, the sections about what we need to continue to do, and what we need to stop and start doing. We often let this ruminate in our hearts and minds for days and weeks.

3. Review the section *What Vision Is and Is Not* in this Re-Visioning workbook as a checkpoint to make sure your vision aligns with God's.

4. For those items that require research, or a "pre-step," or more prayer, take the first step toward doing it today or tomorrow and/or set a deadline. For example:
   - ☐ I will start researching the best way to learn a language. *Tonight online.*
   - ☐ Run the idea past my leadership team. *At Monday's meeting.*
   - ☐ Block off dates for vacation today. *Done.*
   - ☐ Get counsel about my plan. *I called Jen today and set up a time.*
   - ☐ Go over all of this with my spouse/good friend. *Scheduled for Tuesday.*
   - ☐ Pray for 10 days, restart a Bible study. *Started today, Jan 9th.*

_____

_____

_____

_____

_____

_____

_____

_____

_____

_____

_____

_____

_____

_____

_____

_____

_____

_____

_____

_____

_____

_____

_____

5. Schedule Re-visioning for next year. Or schedule it now to carry out with a broader team as soon as possible.

"And all Judah rejoiced . . . for they had sworn
with their whole heart and had sought Him earnestly,
and He let them find Him." (2 Chronicles 15:15 NASB)

What Is High Impact?

In 1992, God called Wendy and Al Newell to start a consulting ministry called Newell and Associates: *High Impact Volunteer Ministry Development.* Since that time, they and their small team have had the privilege to walk alongside leaders as they develop deep-rooted, high-impact (effective) volunteer ministries to the worldwide Body of Christ. High Impact has been taught and applied effectively in more than 100 countries.

Visit www.newellandassociates.com to order additional *Re-visioning* booklets or to learn more about High Impact Volunteer Ministry Development, the Executive Course in Volunteer Ministry Development, or other leadership resources.